Acetylene

Acetylene
poems

Carol Quinn

Winner of the 2008 Cider Press Review Book Award

ACETYLENE

Cider Press Review, LLC
777 Braddock Lane
Halifax, PA 17032, USA
CIDERPRESSREVIEW.COM

First edition
09 9 8 7 6 5 4 3 2 1 0

ISBN: 978-1-930781-05-4
Library of Congress Control Number: 2009936431

Cover art "Death Valley Mud Flat" © James D. Steele /
www.photographybysteele.com.
Author photograph by Carol Quinn.
Cover design by Caron Andregg.

Printed in the United States of America
at BookMobile, in Minneapolis, MN.

CONTENTS

Special Thanks

Special thanks to Adam Zagajewski, Edward Hirsch, Mark Doty, Cynthia MacDonald, Jim Pipkin, David Mikics, Dorothy Baker, David St. John, Michael Theune, Kevin Prufer, Jeneva Stone, Nancy Naomi Carlson, Clarinda Harriss, Ed Duncan, David Bergman, Christoph Irmscher, Harriet Vaugeois, Jeff Paynton, generous grants from Inprint Inc., Caron Andregg and everyone at Cider Press Review, my mother, my grandmother, my aunt, my family, and so many others who have offered their tremendous kindness and unwavering support.

There are no events but thoughts and the heart's hard turning, the heart's slow learning where to love and whom. The rest is merely gossip, and tales for other times.

—Annie Dillard

. . . and at last, God sends each seeker his first fiery thorns.

—Federico García Lorca

Proem

Afterimage

This fuse may weld or wed,
cut or cauterize, as it dissolves
what was. The torch's arc can turn
even steel (slag-sparks excepted)
and persists if submerged —
though the spectacle demands
more than brine or air, more
than that which merely exists —

blinding those it lures.

One

Dark Secret Love

One day in the spring of 1778, David Bushnell, a colonist from what would be Maine, flooded the tanks of a homemade bathysphere to see how long his own breath could sustain him. Only Alexander of Macedonia, who was said to have a diving bell made of glass, had done anything like this before. Bushnell could navigate by cranking propellers, so to save his strength, he gave over to the current for a while. After fifteen minutes, phalanxes of bass glinted around him. Kelp strained against its roots as he passed through. A sea horse held on like his newborn daughter's hand. After forty-five minutes, he saw wrecks still burning under water—the sponges and crinoline leaves like clouds of smoke suspended. He began to dream of the fire hunts of his childhood, the blue flickering in the eyes of baffled deer. Then he felt the impact. He opened the hatch and saw that he had drifted up against a blockade ship.

Only then did he know what he was capable of.

The Promenade

after the painting by Marc Chagall

Every marriage is its own universe.

Each has laws that may defy the logic
of all other systems. Elsewhere,

what little light there is collapses.
Auroral flares are wind across the tops of flues.

But in a certain Lithuanian town,
snow melts and walls turn green in the sun.

What has happened has not yet happened.

The painter's wife appears in a cloisonné
of blowing petals. She has lifted off

and her husband holds her hand
with the grip of a trapeze artist: ready

to follow. He grins with incredible joy.
It's true that someone's poured some wine,

but there is just one glass.

Meanwhile, the green village has begun
to come apart. A chasm splits the town—

but what has happened here cannot be
undone. He thinks he should drink deeply.

He remembers nights when Bella used to climb
out through her bedroom window.

She came to his studio to pose for him.
He'd never seen a naked woman.

Vitebsk was scandalized.

Try and tell them my fiancée is purer
than Raphael's Madonna and I'm an angel.

Elsewhere, too much has happened.
They think they know how the world works.

Such knowledge keeps them down.

Moab

I spent the first night in the ruins
of a filling station. No one passed by.
The silence was like being under water.

In a town where they had
no flag at the founding, they raised
a striped rug woven by a native woman.

They saluted that rug, marching band and all.

In the hollow of a bluff, human forms
were preserved in ochre, though
their hearts had been struck out with stones.

No one knew what their offense
was any longer, or if what bled
from their shoulders were wings or rain.

How much those rocks held of old storms—
like a clock back home with its sound
of water running under boulders.

You asked what it was like. I said nothing,
but collected a vial of that water.
Sometimes the words of love must go unsaid.

One day, hold this page up to your fire.

Apostasy

On Sundays, they appeared
like a recurring dream of flight.
They landed just as church
was getting out. For my mother,
they were missionaries of
a rival creed. They had long hair.
They put faith in the leanings
of their bodies and the air.
She tried to warn me, but I
secretly loved the scaffolds of
their wings. After *cheating death*
(those were her words), their wings
were stolen canvases cut from frames
and quetzals eating from the hand.
She said that no one would be there
to bear me up the day I stepped away,
but that was not the hardest thing.
More difficult than flight itself
was learning how to brace a wing
for someone else—holding to
the wire as if it were a bow—
and then, when he asked me to,
let go.

After Tsvetaeva and Mandelstam

at the Kremlin Cathedral

Each dome supports another. One leans against
the other (as the golden shells inhere),
and these lovers must have walked here once:
a *young Derzhavin* and his *Aurora* in fur.

Each church kept separate hours. Bells relayed
the lingering moment in polyphonies.
A choir felt their voices catch, delayed
within a cupola: a madrigal's slow chase.

How young the singers were. It would not last—
but a cappella, each could still recall
their old harmonic parts (though words were lost)
and sing as if such songs would keep them whole.

And after years and wars and other loves,
the words would fall like snow on unmarked graves.

Deep Sea Dantesca

They'll tell you how they live without the one
thing you thought necessary for all life.
They huddle at their hearthfires and complain.

They miss the break of dawn. Some are bored stiff.
The water neither boils nor turns to ice.
Their children shake their heads in disbelief

at hearing how they learned to bear the press
of the dark element a little more
each day until they felt no emptiness.

For *day*, to those born here, is just old lore.
More constant fire is hedged in by the dark.
They can't imagine any other star.

The old ones sometimes dream of living coral,
the morning sun in tide pools, sea anemones,
how drifting on the current felt euphoric—

but they themselves would never tell you this.
They'd tell you that they're safer where they are.
They'd talk about the fickleness of skies.

Graal

*The Graal technique was developed in Sweden in 1916:
the initial bubble of glass is overlaid with different
layers of crystal glass, coloured or clear depending on
the outcome of the desired and planned design....*

—Ola Höglund and Marie Simberg-Höglund

There are waves
that reach us and waves that we

send out. Layers coalesce
like the rings of trees, mother

of pearl.

The first form is called
a *gather* (though it only smolders

to itself). To shape it,
you will need a potter's patience

and a welder's sense
of urgency.

The object is becoming
That which, at our lips, might heal us—

but if you act too soon,
your work will sag

under its own burning
weight.

14

Hesitate,
and it will shatter in the cold.

Some compare this substance to
the mist that rises from new graves

in that country.

When day returns,
you can't take back your breath.

Hour of Birds

I wake too soon to the lamp's last flutterings.

Nothing can content them.

The crickets' insistence, the rain-gutter doves—

My body is mute in reply.

Tell me, at least, some truth in absentia.

The robin hears only the earth.

The starlings have been swept in with their gale.

They pick at the scraps of the landfill.

I am the same, though everything has changed.

This sentience is only insomnia.

Motorhome Agon

for Julie Reiser

It must sound like something is trying
to be born. At home, they were too far
from their neighbors for anyone to hear.

Their house was like the fossil of an egg.

But their walls are thinner now,
so they're throwing things. They are
like insects trapped together under a glass.

She takes their daughter out into the desert.

The girl will remember petrified wood.
Agate rings flowed from her hands
like ripples across the surface of water.

She'll think of the argument years later
while watching a play by Euripides.

The set is sheet metal loosely sewn
together like hides: ringing skins
that thunder like the walls of a motorhome.

Flint spearheads shatter against bronze
as Diana Rigg pounds home her lines as Medea.

Jason only taps in rebuttal.

A band of light slips across the stage
to signify a day.

◎

But why a day?

As if any tangle of habits and Fatal threads
could be twisted smooth between
the thumb and forefinger of earth and sun.

In the calendar of shadows on the desert,
it's been twenty-five years.
The woman and her daughter walked

until they found the woman couldn't
take off her ring.

The daughter, who has walked out after
another argument, realizes
the ripples might have been returning.

Reversal and recognition:
catharsis comes with the discovery,
There, but for the grace of God ...

She keeps walking toward the vanishing point.

◎

As the others go by, she wonders
at what cost they maintain the illusion—

if it shields them from what thunders,
if they fear the lack of comfort,
or if they have been exiled from Colchis, Corinth,

or Los Angeles with two young sons.

In a parking lot, she listens
for the sound inside, and wonders if
what would be born will ever,

with its own strength,

break from shadows and translucence
to fill its lungs
with the sharp and oxidizing air

where the deer outside her tent sound like soft rain.

Two

Navel-Gazing with a Bullet

Perhaps you were even looking down
in the general direction of that healed wound
through which the blood first divined its ingress

as you sat at your desk, waiting for something
to come to you—though you hardly expected it
to pierce drywall, plaster, and a pane of glass

before vanishing in carpet. You were almost lost
in thought when the tempered glass of your apart-
ment tore open, crumbling back to beach pebbles.

And then you noticed the hole in the ceiling—
the one your friends would finger out of doubt—
like some omphalos connection with the dark.

Street Excavation

They are repaving McClean Boulevard at last,

and even the autumn overcast
is like broken asphalt—

        as if the *hereafter*
were just an echo of the *here* and *now*.

But the dig reveals more about the past—
the tracks and curbs that no one remembers now—

or the winter salt that could ruin someone's fields
or turn the street itself into a primordial sea.

Tar was poured on a summer day
when, just across the street, a boy fell.

Children carried candles as if they were small birds.

Under the glass of bottles, syringes, automobiles

there's a layer of blue, red, and green shards
carefully embedded

        that the street itself
might be beautiful in headlights and rain.

In leaf chaff are remnants of
a pigeon's body, an umbrella, a physics book—

all bonded with asphalt though they try

to lift off in the wind of passing cars.

It's like when you were a child.

Someone held your arms down as
you counted—then let go,

and your arms drifted skyward, out of your control.

Caisson

for Brian Turner

That we might be rootless, ruthless, industrious, dust—

That we might travel far from the places we were born, becoming a new breed—

That we might commute when the shade of reddening leaves is like daylight through closed eyes—

We form a swift tributary. In the valley below, there's the ghost of an inland sea.

On the radio, someone says it would be better if their families acted as though they were already gone—

Everyone is trying to pass a procession of cars.

Some traditions mark an earlier necessity. The wagons that once carried out artillery returned with the dead.

When Whitman tended his wounded, coffins were scarce. The dead were sometimes only wrapped in their banners.

I catch up with the lead car. Through one of its windows, I see a patch of sky.

They are the stars before sunrise.

If the one below that sky returned like Lazarus, he or she would wake in a strange hemisphere, with constellations like legions on parade or graves on a battlefield—

Like orchards in their lines—

He or she might never find the way home.

Everyone keeps passing them, trying to keep moving in the cold.

On the radio, they say *stop loss* as if something could still be saved.

Deep within the combustion engines, matter gives up the ghost like water going over a wall.

Cixi's Headdress

Empress Dowager Cixi ruled China from 1861 to 1908.

No one remembers her name
before she gave the emperor

his only son,

but in her hair, she sometimes wore
the wings of kingfishers.

They were retooled,
                    refashioned—

but still blue

like the evening light
on the other side of curtains

hiding an assassin.

Her son would be taken by smallpox.

She would hold her nephew
                    prisoner

in an island palace on a lake
within the Forbidden City.

He was a reformer
who would die of what no one knew

was arsenic poisoning.

The day after, she herself
would brazenly lie in state

in the Middle Sea Hall of Graceful Bird.

One Stone

They've left their black bread out for us.

There are messages scrawled where wheels once bore down by the brothel.

The sky is clear, but there's still a shadow of ash.

An archaeologist pours plaster into their absence—but we know they are only approximations.

They are wax to be displaced by bronze. They are voices drifting on the airwaves.

They are like cobalt glass. The pupil opens wider to receive the sun.

Pliny wrote, *Laocoön, his children, and the wonderful clasping coils of snakes were carved from a single block ...*

Some would claim the excavated sculpture was the instant perfected, the triumph of *pictura* over *poesis*—like the view from the camera mounted on the coming bomb.

The archaeologist recognizes a hollow and pours more plaster. If the dead are not real for us, what are the living?

The ash is chipped away. See how they refused to leave each other.

His nephew wrote that, when Pliny saw the great cloud spreading its branches over the mountain, he brought a fleet into the harbor.

And then we are blinded. The ash that rained down becomes static. One of these forms could be his.

Old Mattresses

Sometimes you find them in the woods
like sleeping bodies abandoned by their dreamers.

Even out where roads slip from their ligature

and the foundations of mining towns
gaze unblinkingly at the stars,

you find this rusted bullion of coils.

The rush is over. The crowd moved on
when the flickering died out.

Their beds were left to break down in the rain.
Their beds were left for other conflagrations.

Whoever was kept awake by a sound
through the wall like a deathwatch—

Whatever body was withheld from earth—

No matter, now.

When the fire came, the coils poured
from the disintegrating fabric—

writhing in their own dream of flight.

Soliloquies at the Outer Banks

CRO

—*inscription found at the site of the
abandoned colony of Roanoke*

1. *Lost Painting by John White*

Following their feasts and practices, a daughter
of the Picts keeps watch at arms before
the thatch and windmills of our present future.
The stippled flowers of her skin are bare.
Engravers' copies of the painting hint
at what the Roman garrisons saw more
than my soft sketches and unpiercing paint.
A father's gentleness? Adventurer
and expedition artist, I came to lead.
My daughter was among the settlers
at Roanoke. If I idealized
the land, the crops still failed. They found no pearls.
Yet she believed—as if in trees sketched with
the very charcoal left when they'd been razed.

2. *Lost Colony*

Outside, leaves stick. Ragged newsprint clings.
That which preserves, contains—one changed reminds
me: they have flickering, unbroken wings.
They feel their way like human hands.
Now turquoise, teal, indigo in motion—
sometimes they black out deep in their oblique,
then come back like the first light on the ocean.
But underneath, they're rain-soaked bark.
Through masks of branches, eyespots blink and glance
away. Mid-sentence, satellites go dark.
You seemed to see. Windows once meant *eyes*
of wind. The wings' reflective markings are
like windows in a blighted city: blind,
walled-in eyes of wind. *No longer look for me—*

3. *Croatoan*

I waited for a sail to return.

I waited while the cannons rose and gold
was lifted from a dayless depth to shine.

Let this story's ending go untold.

On different shores, we will become
the other's myth: the pearl that forms around
the grain that we remember, a word that named
the meeting place—or syllable that sounded
like a bird that carries fire.
                          The smoke of sand
fills in your tracks (but you gave up the search
too soon). I want to turn back from the sea.
In braids the quartz unravels. Shells will be
chaff shoals, and all will churn and break and wear
to whispering dunes of bitter, blowing sand.

4. Lost Letter

This coast subdues. The currents bank the shards
of what is cast, outcast, endlessly tossed—
and sand collects and passes through like words.

Though you will never hear, I still resist
and write as water fills the hull: a letter
to be found among the amphorae and rust.

We knew our galleon was lost and let
its freight of ponies go. It would be cruel
to make them share in our ship's fate.

Let me go, my love, and grow forgetful.
Unmoor the anchor; cut the astral thread
that runs between us in the darkness like a tether.

The sand reminds me of you. I do not fear
its pale of wrists and lips, its whispered prayer.

5. Assateague

Letting go, the fallen waves pull back
across the gasping surface of the sand.

They leave what they have filched from rock
and wrecks. The low pines fitted to the wind

hold fast as they at last release their sand.
I lose my way. The present has no maps.

How quickly roads and houses are abandoned.
The wind performs its ongoing eclipse.

New forms appear. A head emerges from
the body of the sea. Soon there will be

a band of them reliving their escapes
and passages, their uncut manes half foam

until they stand like newborn foals, shake free,
and gallop from the present's gray collapse.

Sequoia

for Frank

Like the foot of an elephant
that holds up the sky,
its scale recasts everything.
Lightning may not only be
survived, but shrugged off.
80 years is barely long enough
to grow a sturdy branch.
Cities are just petrified forests
before what lives and might recall
Vesuvius, or the night
the Crab Nebula cracked its shell.
But as Niobe was transformed,
perhaps, in the distant past,
they loved and were changed by it.
Perhaps they outlived those
they loved, like a friend of mine
who survived a plague—
although he carried its seeds
like a pinecone to the fire.
Once, he sheltered others like
an ancient, almost immortal thing.
This ash is all that remains.

Radiopacity

1.

At its edge, the asphalt rings
to wake the driver to descansos,
the last mile markers of the dead.
Headlights open the confinement
of the night, revealing sea beds as
the interstate descends, gravel trails
left by railroads pulling back
like glaciers, a low and startled owl.
Once, you waited for me there
beyond the night. We slept
in apartments lit like fire opals
through their dusty windows—
while moths gnawed at the lamps.

2.

Remember through the light and space
where light attends to absence.
When did you first know you'd leapt
into the darkness? On a mountain road,
on the way to see someone
who would become your lover,
who's since relinquished breath you shared,
a bird broke through your high beams.
You never knew for certain if
you grazed those wings, but when you woke,
the morning's lofty whiteness broke apart
like the loose down of an owl's breast.

3.

At seventeen, I drove to Calico,
abandoned underground when all its mines
went bust, to shelter in the earth and seek
a god like silver smelted—or find,
at least, the ore now light with wind.
Instead, there was the casket of a violin
cast off by one last prospector.
Perhaps he came to sound the space
left by the missing—or knew
a fault line in the wear that stripped his bow.
Far above him, constellations drifted,
cut from aching strings. The earth
moved in its sudden time alone.
His lungs now dark, now shuddering
like those rafters, he was past redemption—
but his bow could steal fire from the passing world.

Three

Afterlife

It would have to be a red house—
the kind Jimi Hendrix sang about,
or the common forest cottage that
gets rented on a weekly basis
in Sweden. Brief and mysterious,
the night would bring no dreams except
its own: distant cities, radiant heat.
The door would not keep out the breeze.
Fittingly, the cabinets and walls would be
unfinished pine. T.V. would hint
at human forms through blowing snow. The bed
would have too many quilts, and there'd be
a guest book by the door where someone wrote,
I waited here for you as long as I could.

Gift

Parings of oblivion:
these leavings lifted from the sea.

Driftwood and obsidian slivers
stir, are stirred in turn:

chiming, still, not flaking—
slaking until slack.

There was not time
for the mineral to crystallize,

so it cries more clearly,
with a sheer tone

it might not have had. Listen
(and the windchime is a carillon.

In exile,
the ocean sifts the sand

again and again,
looking for something.

At last, there is no difference between
I do and *I am*.) I will.

Waking in Winter

The way that one might rise
from the Marianas Trench—

leaving behind the anglerfish
unused to all illumination but their own

failing fire....

The way that one might leave
the wreckage of one's loss—

the pocket watches and porcelain faces
that stare and do not change—

against the weight of the delta waters
of the Lethe ....

A thousand miles inland,
a cardinal pecks at a window feeder

and taps at the glass, while the moon—
whose photophores would bruise

against the sway of kelp—washes up
on the shore, still familiar.

Honeymoon at Waitomo Cave, New Zealand

Glow worms wait among stalactites,
casting their lights like anglers in the dark.
Outside, the moths are carried by the breeze.
They follow the river underground and rise
toward what must seem to them like stars.

Night Travel

If only they could sleep
in the same place. Upstairs,
reading in bed, she listened
to the television below,
where he was going to sleep.
There was no argument.
Nothing was said at all
that night, but the jolt
of her body drifting off
was a jet touching down
somewhere else. If only
the bright cities of the desert
still connected to the city
where he was. If only
the old frontiers were nothing
more than synapses. When
they woke, the distance had grown—
but they couldn't remember
when they'd moved apart.

Clizia and Apollo

after Brandeis and Montale

In the silence of these years
I've longed to tell you how your storms
still come to me, the water falling

from the moss in the branches—

how the smoke changed when cars caught fire
under the ruins (in the crowd
someone was already throwing rose petals)—

how we might have kept each other
from despair—

                      but our time is short,
so let me tell you one last story while I can.

A poet loved a woman and called her Clizia—
for a nymph who turned into a sunflower
in her longing—but after she was gone,

he was the one who watched the way that roots
thirst blindly. And he foresaw the trenches.
She couldn't have stayed in Mussolini's Rome.

But the earth—the poet's rival—had
been robbed of its prize. She made it out alive.
Still, he sometimes looked for her—

the way he looked for storm clouds when he heard
the dry, distant thunder of the front.

◎

Years after she left that country, she tried
to translate his words—

but *il tuo piede attutito* became
your muffled step, further muffled

in her own language.

What was lost was like her own loss—
inexpressible; abandoned out of necessity.

Still, she sought him in the words
the way the woman looked for him in "L'orto,"

and she didn't know in whose voice she was speaking
when she wrote,

> *If the force*
> *that turns the disc* already cut
> *were another, your destiny bound up with mine*
> *would show a single groove.*

She could not go back.
But she knew, at least, that he had looked for her

the way that she had sometimes looked for him
when there was no longer any chance that she would find him—

after some other sight—more urgent and blinding—had drawn her gaze
away.

Chaconne

after Bach

The centuries are so much rosin
on the strings,
but grief is still warm,

still there. The wind
draws its bow across the roof.

A dirge recalls
some old exuberance
(this is a dance, after all).

A bow pulls
until its threads can't bear—

then returns, repeating
its unanswerable question.
Some threads have broken free.

When she was
his bride, he told her

that the long, stray hairs he found
were like these threads
snapped in the heat of song.

He still finds them in the house
where something tried to catch her.

Angiogram of a Brain

The rigging of the stranded vessel
glistens against a pure, opaque abyss.

Photos of the *HMS Endurance*
were taken when the ship was sealed in ice

and listing to one side. It's dark—
Antarctic night—but the hull is lit up like

the moon. Who knows what source of light
they had—adrift in pack ice, 1915?

While others prayed for their return—
though no one yet had come back as

they would—perhaps the sailors also felt
the passing, cold aphasia of their place-

lessness when the tautened timbers groaned.
How easily that outpost could go under.

Blossoming Almond Tree

after the painting by Vincent van Gogh

Winter branches also improvise.

I tried to show you, but you said
My hands have gone cold in these years —

then you asked me how I knew it was winter.
I might have said *Your hands —*

©

Winter branches also improvise
in cold light, yearning for saturation.

Survival's no sure thing —
besides, it will only last

so long. Light initiates
a correspondence, a constellation ....

The red pigment darkens the air
in sharp relief.

©

Winter branches also improvise,
though the silence could seal them in ice.

There's no imperative but theirs —

and so the man paints quickly, as if he fears
the blossoms will fall before he's done.

There are risks in waiting for resurrection.

Spinning Wheel

for Becca Keaton

She calls this *threading*
the needle, mixing the gases
until they catch
fire—
     or inflame,
releasing what is already
within (whatever fire is).
The world seems solid in
its artifacts—though
she knows only the surface
is frozen—
        and underneath,
it flows through rusted cans,
corrugation
from some failed shelter,
parts of an old sewing machine—
the wheel going nowhere.

When the small star could pass
through almost anything,

the sculptor takes up her torch.

        ◎

She has no memory of this,
but she's told that it happened.

Once—and possibly more than once—
habit turned against itself.

It bloomed like an opal and
unraveled.

       The nebula expanded,
cracking like a penitent's whip.

The elements would be recast
in the acetylene of a beginning

or an end. The poles kept reversing—
until the day the welder stood

in the schoolyard and let the sun go dark
and watched the playground glow at the seams.

          ◎

At Bethlehem Steel,
it was the start of an epiphanic century.

At the company school,
boys were learning the Bessemer process

and the workers' daughters were learning
to sew.

Everything but marriage
was arranged in advance.

From the coast to the interior
the steel rails rang,
slick with whale oil from the machinery—

and the stars seemed inexhaustible.

◎

The metal yields to a new oblivion
of heat.

With every stitch, what *is* could be
undone, wavering

like some dip-in-the-road mirage.
But she knows there is no other earth,

even if the fire can trace
the wormlike calligraphy of missing threads.

Along the wheel's rim she attaches
an armor of tines she knows
will ring—

like something aeolian
waiting to be touched.

November Aubade

When I was very young, I confused
the sound of crickets with the stars.
It was, almost, a word—the shrill chant diffused
by recurrence. Through the wind the stars
held and wavered. Even now, while walking by
a culvert on a warm November day,
the stagnant water shows a sky—
and the grass is deep with stars. But they
have dimmed—these are the last to fade—
like the voice of someone you once loved
you still hear in the early light of day.

Losing Contact

... we search among ghostly errors of observations
for landmarks that are scarcely more substantial.

—Edwin Hubble, *The Realm of the Nebulae*

The cosmos will go on—albeit like
a piano player in a restaurant
where nobody is listening. Chromatic
nuances will blur into the unison chant
of polite conversation and fluorescent light.
It's just a few black keys, someone will say—
while something miles overhead is set
adrift, and there is silence now where novae
used to pound the bass out underneath the rest.
When hammers strike the strings but no one hears,
the pianist doesn't mind. She is in love
and plays on like a night sky dispossessed.
Just one, one night, need listen to the universe
for that redshifted song to arrive.

Notes

The epigraph from Annie Dillard comes from *Holy the Firm*. The epigraph from Federico García Lorca comes from Ben Belitt's translation of "The Duende: Theory and Divertissement."

The title of the poem "Dark Secret Love" comes from "The Sick Rose" by William Blake.

The italicized lines in "The Promenade" come from *My Life* by Marc Chagall, translated by Elizabeth Abbott and published by Orion Press.

The italicized names in "After Tsvetaeva and Mandelstam" come from both poets' works. *Aurora* is taken from Viktoria Schweitzer's translation of Mandelstam's "In the varied voices of a maidens' choir":

> And the five-domed cathedrals of Moscow
> With their Italian and Russian soul
> Summon up for me the appearance of Aurora,
> But with a Russian name and wearing a fur coat. (129)

Young Derzhavin is taken from Schweitzer's translation of Tsvetaeva's poem, "No one has taken anything away!" (123). Both poems can be found in Viktoria Schweitzer's book, *Tsvetaeva*.

The quote from Pliny the Elder on the Laocoön group comes from D. E. Eichholz's translation of Pliny's *Natural History*, published by Harvard University Press.

Set Fair for Roanoke by David Beers Quinn helped to inform my historical understanding of the colony at Roanoke in "Soliloquies at the Outer Banks."

The italicized passages in "Clizia and Apollo" are taken from "The Orchard" (Irma Brandeis's translation of "L'orto"), which can be found in *The Selected Poems of Eugenio Montale* published by New Directions.

"Chaconne" is a response to J.S. Bach's Chaconne from *Partita No. 2 for Solo Violin in D minor*.

Mark Reutter's *Making Steel: Sparrows Point and the Rise and Ruin of American Industrial Might* provided historical information that was useful in the creation of "Spinning Wheel."

Acknowledgments

Grateful acknowledgment is made to the following journals and publications, in which these poems (some in different versions) have appeared or are forthcoming:

Alaska Quarterly Review: "Afterlife," "Angiogram of a Brain"
American Literary Review: "Gift," "Sequoia"
Anderbo.com: "Graal"
The Bellingham Review: "Chaconne"
The California Quarterly: "Losing Contact"
The Cincinnati Review: "Afterimage," "Caisson," "Spinning Wheel"
Colorado Review: "Motorhome Agon"
Euphony: "November Aubade," "Clizia and Apollo"
Kalliope: "Losing You" (an early version of "Losing Contact")
Many Mountains Moving: "Night Travel"
The National Poetry Review: "Deep Sea Dantesca"
North Carolina Literary Review: "Soliloquies at the Outer Banks"
Open Windows 2005: "After Tsvetaeva and Mandelstam"
Pleiades: "Apostasy," "Old Mattresses"
Puerto del Sol: "Waking in Winter"
River Styx: "One Stone"
The Robinson Jeffers Tor House Foundation Website: "The Promenade"
Verse: "Dark Secret Love," "Radiopacity"
Verse Daily: "Apostasy," "Deep Sea Dantesca"

About the
Cider Press Review Book Award

First Prize: $1,000 and Publication of Book
2009 Judge: David St. John

- Manuscripts can be submitted by mail or online using the entry form at **ciderpressreview.com/bookaward**
- Submit 48-80 pages of original poetry in English not previously published in full-length book form (individual poems may have been previously published in journals, anthologies and chapbooks)
- Manuscripts must be postmarked or submitted online between September 1 and November 30 of the contest year
- For mail submissions, enclose 2 title pages: Name, mailing address, phone number and email should appear on the first title page only
- For online submissions include title page with title of manuscript only
- Manuscript should be typed, single-spaced, paginated and bound with a spring clip
- Include a table of contents page(s) and an acknowledgments page listing previous publication credits
- Enclose an SASE with mailed manuscript for announcement of winner only
- Electronic submissions will be notified via email only
- Include a check or money order for $25 payable to Cider Press Review, or remit entry fee via PayPal
- **Manuscripts cannot be returned**
- All entries will receive a copy of the winning book

Mail to:

Cider Press Review Book Award
777 Braddock Lane
Halifax, PA 17032

For more information, visit **ciderpressreview.com**